AMERICAN
SPACE MISSIONS
ASTRONAUTS, EXPLORATION, AND DISCOVERY

Spacewalk

The Astounding Gemini 4 Mission

Carl R. Green

Enslow Publishers, Inc.
40 Industrial Road
Box 398
Berkeley Heights, NJ 07922
USA
http://www.enslow.com

Original edition published as *The* Gemini 4 *Spacewalk Mission* in 2004.

Library of Congress Cataloging-in-Publication Data

Green, Carl R.
  Spacewalk : the astounding Gemini 4 mission / Carl R. Green.
    p. cm. — (American space missions—astronauts, exploration, and discovery)
  Includes bibliographical references and index.
  Summary: "Explores the *Gemini 4* mission, including the astronauts and the first American spacewalk, the spacecraft and technology that made it possible, and how the *Gemini* mission laid the foundation for the *Apollo* missions to the moon" —Provided by publisher.
  ISBN 978-0-7660-4075-5
  1. Project Gemini (U.S.)—History—Juvenile literature. I. Title.
  TL789.8.U6G358 2013
  629.45'4—dc23
                    2011030869
Future editions:
Paperback ISBN 978-1-4644-0076-6
ePUB ISBN 978-1-4645-0983-4
PDF ISBN 978-1-4646-0983-1

Printed in the United States of America
032012 Lake Book Manufacturing, Inc., Melrose Park, IL
10 9 8 7 6 5 4 3 2 1

To Our Readers: We have done our best to make sure all Internet addresses in this book were active and appropriate when we went to press. However, the author and the publisher have no control over and assume no liability for the material available on those Internet sites or on other Web sites they may link to. Any comments or suggestions can be sent by e-mail to comments@enslow.com or to the address on the back cover.

♻ Enslow Publishers, Inc., is committed to printing our books on recycled paper. The paper in every book contains 10% to 30% post-consumer waste (PCW). The cover board on the outside of each book contains 100% PCW. Our goal is to do our part to help young people and the environment too!

Illustration Credits: James McDivitt / NASA, pp. 8, 10, 26, 27; NASA, pp. 12, 18, 29, 31, 34, 36, 42; NASA Johnson Space Center, pp. 1, 4, 16, 24, 32, 38, 40; NASA Kennedy Space Center, pp. 7, 14, 21; Time & Life Pictures / Getty Images, p. 23.

Cover Illustration: NASA Johnson Space Center (Ed White floats in zero gravity during spacewalk on *Gemini 4* mission).

Contents

CHAPTER 1

An American Spacewalk

The year was 1965. It was the era of the Cold War, a time of intense rivalry between the United States and the Soviet Union. Which system of government would triumph, democracy or communism? In the military realm, the race was on to build more destructive weapons. In science, the challenge lay in blazing new trails in space. The Russians had jumped out in front by launching the first space satellite in 1957. Eight years later, the United States still was playing catch-up.

On June 3, 1965, a Titan II rocket blasted the *Gemini 4* spacecraft into orbit. The ship carried two American astronauts: Command Pilot Jim McDivitt and Pilot Ed White. Ten weeks earlier, the Russian cosmonaut Alexei Leonov had made headlines by taking a ten-minute "walk" in space. Now, as McDivitt ran down the checklist, White was suiting up for his own spacewalk. His bosses at NASA (the National Aeronautics and Space Administration) called it an EVA (Extra Vehicular Activity). Each piece of equipment had been checked and rechecked in the lab. Now, the real test was at hand. Would White's suit and tether safeguard him while he roamed the cold vacuum of space?

Popping the Hatch

After assembling a 7.5-pound (3.4 kilograms) gas gun, White hooked up his 25-foot (7.6 meters) gold-braided tether. Along with providing oxygen, the tether kept him moored to the ship. Next came the emergency oxygen pack. When he finished, McDivitt told Mission Control that all systems checked out. From Houston, the reply flashed back. CapCom (the Capsule Command Communicator) told White, "We're ready to have you get out whenever you're ready."[1]

The astronauts quickly reduced the cabin pressure to zero. White then stood up in his seat and tried to pop the hatch—only to find that it was stuck. When the balky cover did fly open, he had to hold on tight to keep it from banging against the hull. Now, with his head poking out of the hatch, White set up a camera to record his spacewalk. As the world waited, he double-checked his work. "I wanted to make sure I didn't leave the lens cap on," he said later.[2]

Taking Some "Big Steps"

Twelve minutes after popping the hatch, White floated free of the ship. With his eyes shielded from glare by a gold-coated faceplate, he set out to explore his silent world. A pull on the tether sent him looping toward the rear of the ship. A burst from the gas gun brought him back when he came too close to the ship's thrusters. For one confusing moment, White felt as though he was moving in all directions at once. Another burst from the gas gun put him into a controlled turn, and a second jolt stopped the movement. At that point, to the spacewalker's dismay, the gun ran out of gas.[3]

Like his ship, the human satellite sped through space at 17,500 miles (28,158 kilometers) per hour. As he drifted, White described the dazzling earthscape below him. In Houston, Mission Control relayed

Ed White (left) and Jim McDivitt posed for this photo just before the launch of *Gemini 4*. McDivitt piloted the spacecraft into orbit, and White became the first American to "walk" in space.

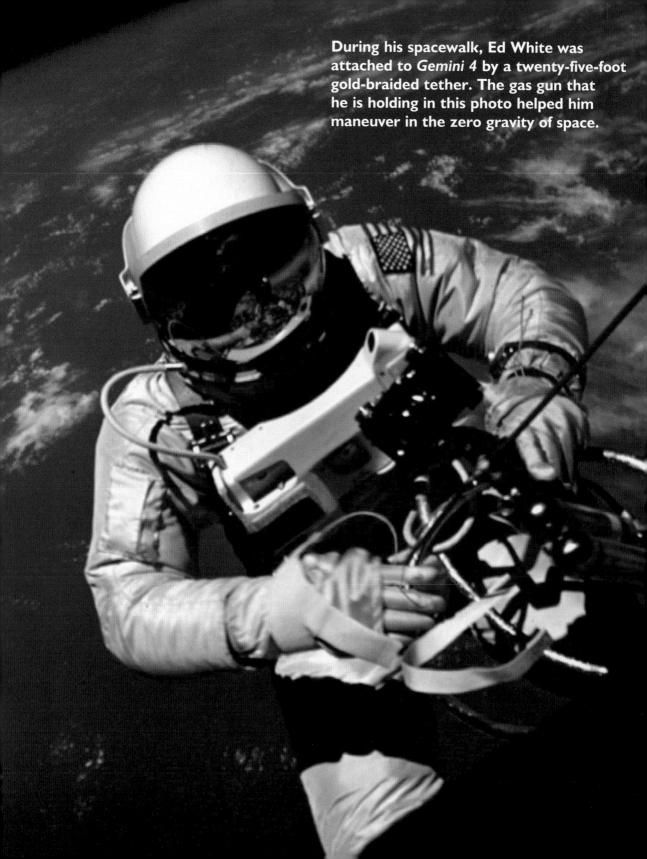

During his spacewalk, Ed White was attached to *Gemini 4* by a twenty-five-foot gold-braided tether. The gas gun that he is holding in this photo helped him maneuver in the zero gravity of space.

his words around the globe. "Right now I'm standing on my head and I'm looking down . . . and I'm going into a slow rotation," he told his spellbound listeners. "There is absolutely no disorientation associated with it. I can sit out here and see the whole California coast."[4] Later, talking to reporters, White recalled, "I was taking some big steps . . . the first on Hawaii, then California, Texas, Florida, and the last on the Bahamas and Bermuda."[5]

Inside *Gemini*, McDivitt had his work cut out for him. "When Ed . . . starts whipping around, it sure makes the craft tough to control," he said. The command pilot also had to be careful not to fire the control thrusters too close to the spacewalker. For his part, White tried to stay out in front of *Gemini*. The tether, however, kept swinging him back toward the rear of the module. At one point, he left smears on McDivitt's windshield when he brushed against it. "You smeared up my windshield, you dirty dog!" his friend said with a laugh.[6]

Time's Up

A hundred miles below, Mission Control watched the clock. By now, White had been in space twice as long as the Russian spacewalker, Alexei Leonov. CapCom told him to end the EVA, but the astronauts were too busy chatting to hear the order. At last, McDivitt asked Houston if there were any messages. The answer came back at once: "*Gemini 4*. Get back in!"

McDivitt relayed the order. "Come on," he told White, "let's get back in here before it gets dark."

This photograph of Ed White was taken during his spacewalk over a cloud-covered Pacific Ocean. White later told reporters about taking "big steps" over Hawaii, California, Texas, and other states and countries.

White knew better than to press his luck. As *Gemini 4* soared high over Georgia, he picked up the camera and unplugged several electrical hookups. Working carefully, he handed his air gun and the other equipment to McDivitt. Then the reluctant astronaut pulled himself back to the hatch.

"It's the saddest moment of my life," White said as he lowered himself into the tiny cabin.[7]

CHAPTER 2

Embarking on a Great Adventure

Ed White's 1965 spacewalk was a much-needed triumph for American science. Four years earlier, the space program had been shaken by some costly launch failures. The Soviet Union's program, by contrast, was roaring ahead. The gap widened again in the spring of 1961. On April 4, cosmonaut Yuri Gagarin became the first man to fly in space. His one-orbit flight, the experts agreed, gave the Soviets a big lead in the space race.

Seven weeks later, on May 25, 1961, President John F. Kennedy stepped forward to address the nation. By then, astronaut Alan Shepard had ridden his *Mercury* capsule into space. Unlike the Soviet flight, NASA's planning had not allowed the capsule to orbit the earth. Shepard's *Freedom 7* splashed down after reaching an altitude of 116 miles (187 kilometers).[1] Even so, President Kennedy used the flight to call for an all-out effort to meet the Soviet challenge. "I believe," the young president told Congress, "that this nation should commit itself to achieving the goal, before this decade is out, of landing a man on the moon and returning him safely to earth."[2]

President John F. Kennedy speaks to Congress on May 25, 1961. In this speech, Kennedy said that he wanted the U.S. space program to land a man on the moon and return him safely to Earth before the end of the decade.

At the time Kennedy spoke, Americans knew that their astronauts had logged only fifteen minutes in space. They also knew that the moon project would cost billions of dollars. In the end, that did not seem to matter. The stirring words inspired the nation to embark on a grand new adventure.

From *Mercury* to *Gemini*

The people who worked on the moon program understood the great obstacles that lay ahead. Step by step, they had to build and test a spacecraft that could carry three astronauts into moon orbit. From there, two crew members would fly a lunar lander to the moon's surface. When their moonwalk was finished, the lander would carry the astronauts back to their mother ship.

NASA began its quest by launching a series of space missions. Each flight was designed to build on the one before. In February 1962, millions cheered as John Glenn rode his *Mercury 6* capsule to a three-orbit flight. Even though the *Mercury* program was far from finished, planners were looking ahead. Next up, they said, would be a larger spacecraft dubbed *Mercury Mark II*.

As the design took shape, NASA changed the *Mark II*'s name to "*Gemini*." The name, Latin for "twins," was inspired by the *Gemini* constellation and its twin stars, Castor and Pollux. In ancient times, the two stars had been known as the patron gods of voyagers. The "twins" label also took note of *Gemini*'s two-man crews. A foot longer and a foot wider than *Mercury*, *Gemini*'s cabin was a full 50 percent larger.[3] No longer a "flying rock" like *Mercury*, the ship's thrusters would allow it to maneuver in space. The design pleased the newly-chosen *Gemini* astronauts. The new spacecraft would allow them to do what they were paid to do—fly.[4]

Long before the first ship reached the launchpad, NASA had approved a bold set of goals. If all went as planned, the *Gemini* teams would tackle six tasks:

- Test the effects of prolonged spaceflight on both the crew and the spacecraft.
- Check out crew rest and work cycles, eating schedules, and real-time flight planning.
- Test EVA equipment and procedures.
- Rendezvous and dock with a second space vehicle.

Early space missions in the moon program featured the *Mercury* rocket. Astronaut John Glenn rode his *Mercury 6* capsule to a three-orbit flight. This photo shows an earlier launch of the *Mercury-Redstone 2* carrying the chimpanzee Ham into space on January 31, 1961.

- Maneuver the ship in space and hit a precise landing point during the spacecraft's reentry.
- Carry out scientific experiments.[5]

By the time *Gemini 4* soared skyward, the project was closing in on all of these goals.

Training the *Gemini* Astronauts

NASA set high standards when it picked the *Gemini* astronauts. As with *Mercury*, only young, well-trained test pilots could hope to be chosen. Test pilots, NASA believed, had the skills needed to fly a spacecraft. Each candidate also had to have a college degree in engineering or one of the physical sciences. Without this training, the astronauts would find it hard to communicate with the project's engineers and scientists. Height was also a factor. Because the cockpit was a tight fit, no one taller than six feet could apply. As a final hurdle, the volunteers had to pass a series of tough physical exams.[6]

In 1962, nine *Gemini* astronauts were chosen from over two hundred candidates. A second group of fourteen joined them a year later. Once chosen, the astronauts plunged into their rigorous training program. Long, tough sessions in flight simulators filled many of their days. The mock flights tested the astronauts' responses to problems that could crop up during a mission. One moment, cabin pressure would drop. The next, the guidance system would break down. Astronaut Gus Grissom later wrote about the training, "All of us who flew the *Gemini*

Gemini astronauts John Young (right) and Gus Grissom (left) perform splashdown training exercises in a pool at Ellington Air Force Base, Texas. Grissom said the actual spaceflights were easier than the months of rigorous training that the astronauts had to undergo.

missions are pretty well agreed that the actual flights themselves seemed a lot easier than the simulations 'flown'. . . on the ground."[7]

The training did not stop there. High-speed dives in Air Force transports gave the astronauts brief tastes of weightlessness. The teams also simulated life in zero gravity by working underwater in diving gear. Like the *Mercury* capsule, *Gemini* was designed to splash down at sea. If the spacecraft sank, the astronauts had to know how to escape. Once free of the ship, they had to prove that they could handle a life raft.

Planners also worried that a mishap could force the spacecraft to land far off track. One week the astronauts were set down in the desert, the next in a jungle. Each new "crash" site tested their survival skills.

Gemini 4 Gets a Crew

After long months of training, NASA chose the *Gemini* teams. No one would mistake the two Air Force majors picked to fly *Gemini 4* for twins, but the men were a good fit. Born within six months of each other, James A. "Jim" McDivitt and Edward H. "Ed" White II were the same height. Each man had a wife named Pat. After meeting at the University of Michigan in 1959, both trained as test pilots. McDivitt had flown combat missions in Korea, but White had logged more hours of flying time. In their spare time, both men enjoyed handball, golf, and swimming. As White put it, "Jim and I have been following right along together."[8]

In other ways, the two men were quite different. McDivitt was born in Chicago; White was born in San Antonio. The McDivitts had four children; the Whites had two. White came from a military family and was a West Point graduate. After serving in Korea, McDivitt had gone on to earn his college degree in aeronautics. As an astronaut, he played a key role in designing *Gemini*'s guidance system. White took on the task of making sure the control system had a "pilot's touch." In 1962, each simulator was fitted with a different control stick. Think ahead to the moon missions, White cautioned. Why should astronauts be forced to use one kind of stick to get there and a second to land the lunar module?

Ed White (left) and Jim McDivitt inside the *Gemini 4* spacecraft wait for liftoff on June 3, 1965. With years of experience as test pilots behind them, the two Air Force officers were well qualified to fly the historic mission.

The NASA designers listened—and equipped all American spacecraft with the same control stick.[9]

When White was twelve, his pilot father allowed him to fly an old T-6 trainer. That first turn at the controls helped shape the boy's life. Years later, astronaut Ed White talked about the lesson he learned that day. "Set a goal," he said, "believe in your heart and soul that you can achieve it—and then work to accomplish it."[10]

CHAPTER 3

A Lesson in Orbital Physics

The long weeks of training ended at last. Early on the morning of June 3, 1965, Ed White and Jim McDivitt sat down to their preflight breakfast. While they ate steak and eggs, Cape Kennedy's launchpad LC-19 was buzzing with activity. Inside *Gemini*, the backup crew checked the ship's systems. Out on the pad, the ground crew pumped fuel into a giant Titan II rocket. By 7:07 A.M., the Titan was ready to go. When White and McDivitt climbed into the spacecraft, their silvery space suits gleamed in the morning light.[1] Each suit displayed an American flag patch—a first for the space program.[2]

Around the world, television viewers hurried to turn on their sets. For the first time, a space launch was being broadcast live via Early Bird satellite, which allowed events filmed in North America to be viewed in Europe and around the globe. *Gemini 4*, the news reports promised, would score several "firsts." Space fans knew that this would be the first mission run from the new Mission Control Center in Houston. For the general public, Ed White's EVA was the big draw. NASA's approach to spaceflight was also on display. The Soviets used automated systems to fly their capsules. Cosmonauts never took over the controls unless a major system failed. By contrast, NASA trusted the skills of its former test pilots. *Gemini* astronauts were expected to take a hands-on role in flying their spacecrafts.[3]

Gemini Blasts Off

Only a single glitch marred the countdown. At thirty-five minutes before launch, the erector structure stuck while it was being lowered. Raised to its full height and lowered again, the erector jammed a second time. After a seventy-minute search, workers found and replaced a faulty connector. This time the erector lowered as planned. *Gemini 4* was ready.

The Titan II rocket ignited with a burst of bright orange flame at 10:16 A.M. Riding atop the powerful booster, *Gemini 4* blasted skyward. Inside the nearly silent cabin, McDivitt and White could feel their spacecraft gathering speed. Then, without warning, the rocket began to bounce like a pogo stick. In Houston, the flight controllers held their breath. If the bouncing continued, the rocket might break apart. Then, in the next instant, the "pogoing" stopped as quickly as it had begun. Everyone in Mission Control sighed with relief.[4]

Five and a half minutes after liftoff, *Gemini 4* coasted into its planned orbit. At its apogee (highest point), the spacecraft was 175 miles (282 kilometers) above Earth. The perigee (low point) checked

Gemini 4 blasts off at 10:16 A.M. on June 3, 1965. After a brief delay due to a faulty piece of equipment, the launch went smoothly.

out at 100 miles (161 kilometers). By this time, the booster's engines had cut off as planned. Twenty seconds later, McDivitt punched in the order to separate. As his ship pulled free, he used his thrusters to steer clear of the giant booster. A few minutes later, White spotted their fellow traveler about a hundred yards (91 meters) away. As called for in the flight plan, the astronauts set out to simulate a docking maneuver.[5]

Losing Ground by Flying Faster

NASA's planners assumed that with the booster moving at a constant speed, *Gemini 4* could catch it by speeding up. Now, faced with a real space chase, all the old thinking went out the window. Their quarry, McDivitt and White reported, was tumbling along in a different orbit. If they moved in too close, they might crash into the booster. Despite the risk, the astronauts did their best to catch their target. Using thrusters to gain speed, they chased the booster toward their first dawn in space. Then, as the sun rose in a beautiful rainbow of colors, McDivitt called in a surprising report. The booster, he said, was farther away than ever.[6]

Moments later, the command pilot reported a new problem. "It's taken a little more fuel than we had anticipated," he told Mission Control. "Do you want me to really make a major effort to close . . . or to save the fuel?" The response came back almost at once. "I think we should save the fuel . . . I don't think it's worth it," Mission Director Chris Kraft said. McDivitt hated to give up the chase, but he knew the order made sense. "I'd like to save enough [fuel] to help bring me down," he told Kraft.[7]

NASA employees work in the Mission Control Center in Houston during the flight of *Gemini 4*. When the spacecraft burned too much fuel trying to catch the booster rocket, Mission Director Chris Kraft called off the chase to save fuel for *Gemini*'s return trip.

In Houston, NASA engineers tackled the problem of the elusive booster. Speed and motion in orbit, they decided, do not follow earthly rules. In space, adding speed lifts the spacecraft into a higher orbit. When that happens, the faster-moving ship falls farther and farther behind. Like a runner who takes the outside lane, *Gemini* lost ground because the higher the orbit, the longer it takes to circle the earth. The target vehicle, following a lower (and shorter) orbit, pulls farther and farther away. In later flights, *Gemini* pilots closed on their targets by dropping into lower, not higher, orbits. Only when they moved in close did they apply a burst of power. This final thrust allowed the chase ship to close in and dock with its target.[8]

Floating in Space

After failing to catch the booster, the astronauts turned to their next challenge—the EVA. As White assembled the gas gun, McDivitt went over the lengthy checklist. The first task done, White worked on the hookups for his tether and oxygen pack. As the minutes flew

As *Gemini 4* flew over the Indian Ocean, Ed White opened the hatch and stepped into the inky blackness of space.

by, McDivitt noticed that his partner was looking tired. It would be safer, he thought, to postpone the spacewalk for another orbit. With Houston's okay, the astronauts took a break.

As *Gemini 4* soared over the Indian Ocean, White said he was ready. After struggling with the balky hatch cover, he set up his camera and floated into space. Like all astronauts, he was aware of the danger. If he blacked out, it was unlikely that McDivitt would be able to reel him back into the ship. In that case, the command pilot had orders to cut the spacewalker loose so he could seal the hatch. Buzz Aldrin, who would one day walk on the moon, explained the astronaut's feelings about risk. "We never believed we were doing anything extraordinarily dangerous," he said. "[We] were confident in our ability to do the job for which we were exceedingly well trained."[9]

After exhausting his gas gun, White used the tether to move around the spacecraft. "Changing my position by pulling on the tether was easy, like pulling a trout . . . out of a stream," he said later.[10] Inside the cabin, the tugs on the tether were keeping McDivitt busy.

The suit was working well, and the helmet visor did a good job of shielding White's face from the sun's glare. "I can sit here and see the whole California coast," he told his worldwide audience. From inside the ship, McDivitt snapped photos of the spacewalker as he floated past. Clearly, White was having a great time. "I'm very thankful in having the experience to be first," the spacewalker said. "This is fun!"[11]

All too soon, the order came to end the spacewalk. White pulled himself back to the ship and climbed through the hatch. Closing the cover

Ed White's gold-coated visor did a good job protecting him from the sun's glare.

should have been a simple task, but the stubborn latch again refused to work properly. The long tether, coiling around the cabin like a snake, made the task even more difficult. When White pulled harder, the effort lifted him out of his seat. To aid him, McDivitt reached over, grabbed his legs, and held on tight. As White fought with the cover, his pulse rate climbed to 178 beats a minute. Finally, the latch snapped shut. White dropped into his seat, tired and sweaty—but supremely happy.

In Houston, the controllers took stock of the situation. The flight plan had called for the astronauts to reopen the hatch so they could toss out the EVA equipment. After the battle with the faulty latch, that seemed too risky. CapCom told White and McDivitt they would have to live with the tether and the rest of the gear for the next three days.

Ed White's spacewalk lasted for twenty-three minutes. The return to the capsule, he later said, was the "saddest moment" of his life. This photo shows White floating in space as *Gemini 4* passes over California.

CHAPTER 4

"Pride, Patriotism, and American Know-How"

With *Gemini 4* buttoned up tight, McDivitt took a good look at his partner. White's faceplate, he saw, was fogged with sweat. The sight convinced him that they both needed a rest. In Houston, a big sigh of relief had echoed through Mission Control when the hatch snapped shut. Three teams were keeping a round-the-clock watch on the spacecraft. White Team leader Gene Kranz summed up the pride everyone was feeling. "This was one of those magical moments," he wrote. "Pride, patriotism, and American know-how triumphed that day. I was happy and proud, almost giddy, but then . . . it was time to get back to business."[1]

In the media center, reporters hurried to file their stories. A few spiced up their efforts by calling the ship Little Eva—a tribute to the nation's first EVA. Until this time, each capsule had been given its own

GEMINI

EXTRAVEHICULAR

SPACE SUIT

UNDERWEAR

COMFORT LAYER

PRESSURE BLADDER

RESTRAINT LAYER
(LINK NET)

BUMPER LAYERS HT-1

ALUMINIZED THERMAL
LAYER

FELT LAYER HT-1

OUTER LAYER HT-1

Although both astronauts wore G4C space suits, White's had an extra EVA layer to protect him during his spacewalk. However, once he returned to the spacecraft's cabin, the extra insulation kept him too warm. This diagram shows the suit's different layers.

flight name. John Glenn made the first orbital flight in *Friendship 7*. *Gemini 3* had been christened the *Molly Brown*. McDivitt and White had wanted to call their ship *American Eagle*, but NASA refused. Naming the capsules, officials said, detracted from the serious nature of the missions.[2]

Life in Orbit

After a short rest, the *Gemini 4* astronauts settled into a regular routine. Both men wore their G4C space suits throughout the mission. The suits protected the astronauts from radiation from the sun, as well as sudden changes in cabin temperature and pressure. With the cabin temperature holding at 75°F (24°C), McDivitt said he felt fine. White's suit, with its extra EVA layer, kept him a bit too warm. Six hours into the flight, both men complained of a strong odor that made their eyes burn. Mission Control guessed that the climate-control system was releasing the fumes. Later, the astronauts grumbled about their radio headsets. The lightweight headsets worked well enough—except when they floated off their heads at odd moments.[3]

On shorter flights, astronauts had shown some loss of muscle strength. Worried that the loss might be greater on a longer mission, doctors added a workout program for *Gemini 4*. The exerciser was a bungee cord with a handle at one end and a foot strap at the other. Nothing else would have worked in the tiny cabin. When the astronauts exercised, data flowed back to Houston from sensors embedded in their suits. The sensors kept track of pulse rates, blood pressure, and other vital signs. By the two-day mark, both men told CapCom they had lost interest in their workouts. They were more faithful in doing the stretching routines that relieved cramped leg and back muscles.[4]

For this first four-day flight, sleep and meal breaks had been added to the schedule. The plan was for one man to sleep while the other carried on his duties. But when put to the test, the sleep schedule failed on all counts. Each time the on-duty astronaut moved, he disturbed the sleeper. To make matters worse, the cabin was anything but quiet. The radio crackled, thrusters fired with a whoosh, and power circuits hummed and buzzed. On later *Gemini* missions, the astronauts slept and ate at the same time.[5]

In this photo, packages of beef and gravy (top left) are ready to be "cooked." To prepare their meals aboard the spacecraft, the astronauts squirted water into the dried food packets using the water gun (top right).

The flight plan also called for four meals a day. "Cooking" mostly consisted of squirting water into packets of dried foods. To eat pot roast or chicken, the men squeezed the mushy mix into their mouths through a feed tube. The tastiest dish, they agreed, was smoked bacon. White, who loved big, juicy steaks, had to be content with this menu on the third day:

- *Breakfast*—sugar-toasted flakes, sausage patties, cinnamon toast, orange-grapefruit juice.

- *Lunch*—beef and gravy, cheese sandwich, apricot pudding, orange juice.

- *Dinner*—beef pot roast, green peas, toasted bread cubes, pine-apple cubes, tea.

- *Late dinner*—Chicken bites, toast, applesauce, brownies, grapefruit juice.[6]

To prevent dehydration, doctors asked the men to drink at least two quarts (1.9 L) of fluids a day. At one point, the men's wives joined the doctors in urging their husbands to "drink up." Speaking from Mission Control, Pat White told Ed, "Have a drink of water."

"Roger," the dutiful husband replied. "Stand by for a drink of water."

Moments later, a second voice crackled through the headphones. "Hey, have a drink of water, both of you," Pat McDivitt ordered.[7]

Patricia McDivitt (left) and Patricia White speak to their husbands during the _Gemini 4_ mission as the astronauts pass over the United States. Both wives ordered their husbands to drink more water. Doctors had warned the astronauts that they needed to drink at least two quarts of water a day to stay hydrated.

The two Pats did not know that the men had not bothered to shave or brush their teeth. If they had known, they might have added a few commands about personal hygiene.

Experiments and Observations

As the hours passed, the astronauts met another hazard of life in zero gravity. Each time a juice packet leaked, the droplets floated around the cabin. When they dug into a storage locker, the contents were sure to drift out. That meant catching each object (a gauge or a wrench, perhaps) and stowing it away again. If someone left a locker open, everything floated out all over again.

As the hours ticked by, McDivitt and White carried out a series of experiments. A dosimeter checked on radiation in the capsule. A magnetometer measured changes in the earth's magnetic fields. Another assignment called on their camera skills. As they passed over the United States, the astronauts snapped pictures of the landscape below. One set of photos gave weather experts a topside look at a major storm system. Turning their gaze skyward, the pilots used a sextant to check their position. A sextant measures the angular distance between two points in space, such as the sun and the horizon. The test confirmed that future crews could one day use sextants to help find their way to the moon and back.[8]

Around and above them, the *Gemini* twins glimpsed satellites and burned-out rockets. Looking down, they spotted Egypt's Nile River and the cities of Cairo and Alexandria. White said he could make out

This photo shows the Nile River Delta, Egypt, the Suez Canal, Israel, Jordan, Syria, Saudi Arabia, and Iraq from the *Gemini 4* spacecraft. White and McDivitt reported that they could see details, such as cities, rivers, roads, and airfields, as they orbited the Earth.

roads, streetlights, airfields, and smoke from factory chimneys. These sightings surprised the experts. Most had doubted that astronauts could see such small details from space.[9]

"Like a Falling Rock"

As *Gemini 4* logged a record fourth day in space, CapCom ordered the crew to prepare for reentry. By now, McDivitt had shown that he could maneuver *Gemini 4* with great precision. All seemed ready for him to fly the spacecraft to a gliding reentry. To do so, however, he needed the help of the ship's onboard computer. This was a first for an American spacecraft, and skeptics had warned that it might not work. The computer did work just fine—until day four. At that crucial moment, no matter how the men jiggled the switch, the computer did not respond. The failure left McDivitt with no choice but to make a plunging, *Mercury*-type reentry. To the command pilot, that was like riding a falling rock back to Earth. "I just think it's old fashioned," he muttered.[10]

During orbit sixty-two, the astronauts fired *Gemini*'s retro-rockets. After plunging to an altitude of 16.8 miles (27 kilometers), McDivitt slowed the roll rate and deployed the drogue parachute. A drogue parachute is designed to quickly slow objects as they fall.

Gemini 4 twisted and turned until the main chute popped open and further slowed the descent. Moments later, the ship splashed into the ocean. The impact slammed the two men around a bit, but they were down safely.

A navy frogman team keeps the *Gemini 4* spacecraft afloat as it waits to be hauled aboard the USS *Wasp*. The astronauts boarded a chopper for the ride back to the *Wasp* after leaving the spacecraft.

Due to the computer breakdown, the astronauts landed 50 miles (80 kilometers) short of their target. Helicopters from the USS *Wasp*, however, reached them moments after splashdown. As *Gemini* bobbed in the waves, divers attached a flotation collar to keep it from sinking. McDivitt and White popped the hatch, jumped out, and climbed into a chopper. When they landed on the *Wasp*, the sailors rolled out a red carpet. The warm welcome, White said later, left him feeling "red, white, and blue all over."[11]

CHAPTER 5

"A Long Stride Forward"

Soon after White and McDivitt reached the *Wasp*, the captain called them to the phone. President Lyndon Johnson was on the line. "What you have done will never be forgotten," Johnson told them. "[You] two outstanding men have taken a long stride forward in mankind's progress."[1] To the American people, that "long stride forward" meant that the United States had jumped into the lead in the space race with the Soviet Union.

Before the astronauts left the *Wasp*, doctors ran them through a series of tests. The effects of weightlessness had been the doctors' greatest worry. A few had predicted that the pilots would faint—or even die—when they returned to Earth. To their surprise, neither astronaut showed signs of distress. Except for feeling tired and hungry, they were in good shape. White even danced a little jig when he stepped onto the red carpet. The tests did show that both men had lost some bone mass, but that was expected. Doctors also noted the fact that they had lost weight and their blood pressure had dropped.[2]

Ed White (left) and Jim McDivitt listen to President Lyndon B. Johnson as he congratulates them after their successful mission. Johnson said that what the two men had done "will never be forgotten."

Four days in space left the astronauts badly in need of a shower. As White said with a smile, "I thought I smelled fine. It was all those people on the carrier that smelled strange."[3] While the tests dragged on, the astronauts found it hard to contain their high spirits. At one point, while lying on an X-ray table, McDivitt cut loose with a loud "Yahoo!"[4] On the second day, White joined in a tug-of-war between the ship's sailors and marines. His team lost, but his display of strength and endurance pleased the doctors.[5]

A Nearly Flawless Flight

With medical worries laid to rest, NASA drew up its balance sheet. *Gemini 4*, the record showed, met all but two of its objectives. Early in the flight, lack of fuel cut short the attempt to rendezvous with the booster. Four days later, the computer glitch kept McDivitt from flying the ship to a gliding reentry. As a joke, reporters gave the team an abacus (an ancient, handheld counting device). Use it, they said, if the computer conks out on future flights.[6]

For the most part, both men and machine performed flawlessly. At Mission Control, *Gemini 4*'s support teams proved they were ready to handle longer flights. While in orbit, the astronauts devoted twenty-two hours to eleven important experiments.[7] The high point, clearly, was White's spacewalk. His trouble-free EVA proved that astronauts could do useful work in space. The next big challenge, NASA's engineers agreed, would be the *Apollo* moon mission. After *Apollo*, their dream was to use spacewalkers to assemble an orbiting space platform.

Back in Houston, the astronauts' families welcomed them with smiles and hugs. President Johnson pinned medals on both men and promoted them to lieutenant colonel. Then he sent them to represent the United States at the Paris Air Show. In France, Soviet cosmonaut Yuri Gagarin, revered as the first man to fly in space, shared the spotlight with the *Gemini* twins.[8] When White and McDivitt returned home,

After the astronauts passed all the necessary medical tests, they were awarded with medals, parades, and honorary degrees. Jim McDivitt (left, holding photo) and Ed White (right) stand with President Johnson (center) as he presents photos of the spacewalk.

Chicago honored them with a ticker-tape parade. Not to be outdone, the University of Michigan gave them honorary doctorate degrees. Their new degrees entitled the astronauts to be called Dr. White and Dr. McDivitt.

Opening Doors to the Future

Gemini 4 set a bundle of new space records, from total flight time to time spent in EVA. Then, one by one, those records began to tumble.

Each new *Gemini* mission pushed ahead, building on what earlier flights had achieved. By the time *Gemini 12* splashed down in November 1966, the United States was well out in front in the space race. President Johnson spoke of these successful flights when he said, "Ten times in . . . the last twenty months we have placed two men in orbit . . . ten times we have brought them home."[9] Thanks to *Gemini*, NASA was ready to push ahead with the *Apollo* moon lander program.

Ed White and Jim McDivitt saw the *Apollo* missions as their ticket for more trips into space. For White, that assignment ended in tragedy. On January 27, 1967, he joined Gus Grissom and Roger Chaffee in the command module of *Apollo 1*. During the countdown, an electric spark started an intensely hot fire in the cabin. A few seconds later, all three astronauts were dead. NASA went back to the drawing board to rethink its safety rules.[10]

McDivitt returned to space on March 3, 1969, as *Apollo 9*'s command pilot. During their ten days in Earth orbit, McDivitt, Rusty Schweickart, and Dave Scott gave the lunar module a tough workout. The big test came on their fifth day in space. McDivitt and Schweickart backed the fragile-looking lunar module clear of the *Apollo 9* command ship and flew off into the inky blackness. After simulating an ascent from the moon's surface, they returned to Scott in the command ship. As the docking mechanism snapped into place, cheers erupted in Houston's control center. All the pieces were in place. It was only a matter of time before a team of astronauts landed on the moon.[11]

The *Apollo 9* mission was the final test before **NASA** sent astronauts to land on the moon. **Jim McDivitt was part of the *Apollo 9* crew. In this photo, McDivitt (right) and David Scott take part in a test of the spacecraft.**

Six months later, *Apollo 11* carried Neil Armstrong, Buzz Aldrin, and Michael Collins on their historic moon mission. On July 20, Armstrong and Aldrin flew the lunar lander to a soft landing on the moon.

"Houston, Tranquility Base here. The Eagle has landed," Armstrong told a waiting world.[12] Without a doubt, it was *Apollo*'s show. Back on Earth, however, the *Gemini* crews must have felt that they, too, were part of that great moment.

Chapter Notes

Chapter 1. An American Spacewalk

1. Peter Bond, *Heroes in Space: From Gagarin to Challenger* (New York: Basil Blackwell, Inc., 1987), p. 90.

2. Ibid.

3. Anthony J. Cipriano, *America's Journeys Into Space: The Astronauts of the United States* (New York: Julian Messner, 1979), p. 32.

4. Bond, p. 91.

5. David J. Shayler, *Gemini: Steps to the Moon* (Chichester, UK: Praxis Publishing, 2001), p. 277.

6. Ibid., p. 278.

7. Gene Kranz, *Failure Is Not an Option: Mission Control From Mercury to Apollo 13 and Beyond* (New York: Simon & Schuster, 2000), p. 140.

Chapter 2. Embarking on a Great Adventure

1. Patrick J. Walsh, *Echoes Among the Stars: A Short History of the U.S. Space Program* (Armonk, N.Y: M. E. Sharpe, 2000), p. 22.

2. Ibid., p. 13.

3. Peter Bond, *Heroes in Space: From Gagarin to Challenger* (New York: Basil Blackwell, Inc., 1987), p. 83.

4. United Press International, *Gemini; America's Historic Walk in Space* (Englewood Cliffs, N.J.: Prentice-Hall, Inc., 1965), chapter 1.

5. "*Gemini 4; 1st American Space Walk,*" *Mission History; Detailed Account of the Gemini IV Mission,* May 10, 2000, <http://www.thespaceplace.com/history/Gemini/gemini04.html> (December 5, 2002).

6. Virgil "Gus" Grissom, *Gemini: A Personal Account of Man's Venture into Space* (New York: The Macmillan Company, 1968), pp. 86–87.

7. Ibid., p. 84.

8. Mary C. Zornio, "Detailed Biographies of Apollo I Crew—Ed White," *NASA History,* February 3, 2003, <http://www.nasa .gov/office/pao/History/Apollo204/zorn/white.htm> (April 11, 2003).

9. Ibid.

10. Ibid.

Chapter 3. A Lesson in Orbital Physics

1. Barton C. Hacker and James M. Grimwood, "Four Days and a 'Walk'," *On the Shoulders of Titans: A History of Project Gemini*, n.d., <http://www.hq.nasa.gov/office/pao/History/Sp-4203/ch11-2.htm>, (April 11, 2003).
2. Timothy B. Benford and Brian Wilkes, *The Space Program Quiz & Fact Book* (New York: Harper & Row, Publishers, 1985), p. 53.
3. Patrick J. Walsh, *Echoes Among the Stars: A Short History of the U.S. Space Program* (Armonk, N.Y.: M. E. Sharpe, 2000), p. 15.
4. Gene Kranz, *Failure Is Not an Option: Mission Control From Mercury to Apollo 13 and Beyond* (New York: Simon & Schuster, 2000), p. 137.
5. Ibid.
6. United Press International, *Gemini: America's Historic Walk in Space* (Englewood Cliffs, N.J.: Prentice-Hall, Inc., 1965), chapter 2.
7. Ibid.
8. Hacker and Grimwood.
9. Dr. Fred Kelly, *America's Astronauts and Their Indestructible Spirit* (Blue Ridge Summit, Pa.: Tab Books, Inc., 1986), p. vii.
10. Peter Bond, *Heroes in Space: From Gagarin to Challenger* (New York: Basil Blackwell, Inc., 1987), p. 83.
11. Mary C. Zornio, "Detailed Biographies of Apollo I Crew—Ed White," *NASA History*, February 3, 2003, <http://www.nasa.gov/office/pao/History/Apollo204/zorn/white.htm> (April 11, 2003).

Chapter 4. "Pride, Patriotism, and American Know-How"

1. Gene Kranz, *Failure Is Not an Option: Mission Control From Mercury to Apollo 13 and Beyond* (New York: Simon & Schuster, 2000), p. 139.
2. Barton C. Hacker and James M. Grimwood, "Four Days and a 'Walk'," *On the Shoulders of Titans: A History of Project Gemini*, n.d., <http://www.hq.nasa.gov/office/pao/History/Sp-4203/ch11-2.htm> (April 11, 2003).
3. David J. Shayler, *Gemini: Steps to the Moon* (Chichester, UK: Praxis Publishing, 2001), p. 205.
4. Ibid.
5. Peter Bond, *Heroes in Space: From Gagarin to Challenger* (New York: Basil Blackwell, Inc., 1987), p. 93.
6. United Press International, *Gemini: America's Historic Walk in Space* (Englewood Cliffs, N.J.: Prentice-Hall, Inc., 1965), chapter 4.
7. Ibid.
8. Mark Wade, *Gemini 4*, June 26, 2002, <http://www.astronautix.com/flights/gemini4.htm> (April 11, 2002).

9. Bond, p. 93.

10. United Press International, chapter 4.

11. Timothy B. Benford and Brian Wilkes, *The Space Program Quiz & Fact Book* (New York: Harper & Row, 1985), p. 23.

Chapter 5. "A Long Stride Forward"

1. United Press International, *Gemini: America's Historic Walk in Space* (Englewood Cliffs, N.J.: Prentice-Hall, Inc., 1965), chapter 4.

2. Peter Bond, *Heroes in Space: From Gagarin to Challenger* (New York: Basil Blackwell, Inc., 1987), p. 94.

3. Mary C. Zornio, "Detailed Biographies of Apollo I Crew—Ed White," *NASA History*, February 3, 2003, <http://www .nasa.gov/office/pao/History/Apollo204/zorn/white.htm> (April 11, 2003).

4. United Press International, chapter 4.

5. David J. Shayler, *Gemini: Steps to the Moon* (Chichester, UK: Praxis Publishing, 2001), p. 206.

6. Bond, p. 94.

7. Shayler, p. 338.

8. Zornio.

9. Shayler, p. 399.

10. Bond, p. 139.

11. Chris Kraft, *Flight: My Life in Mission Control* (New York: Dutton, 2001), pp. 305–306.

12. James Schefter, *The Race: The Complete True Story of How America Beat Russia to the Moon* (New York: Anchor Books, 2000), p. 286.

Glossary

Apollo—The series of missions which climaxed when the *Apollo 11* astronauts landed on the surface of the moon.

CapCom—The communications specialist who relays information between Mission Control and the flight crew during a space mission.

extra vehicular activity (EVA)—An activity carried on outside of a space vehicle; spacewalking, for example.

gas gun—A device that fires a jet of compressed gases to help an astronaut control his or her movements during a spacewalk.

hatch—Doors on a spacecraft that allow astronauts to move in and out of the spacecraft, or between separate pressurized compartments. When closed, hatches are sealed to keep the spacecraft pressurized.

Mission Control Center—A room filled with computers and communications equipment where flight controllers monitor spaceflights.

orbit—The circular path of one celestial body or artificial satellite around another.

reentry—The phase of a spaceflight during which astronauts pilot their spacecraft through Earth's atmosphere to their landing site.

tether—A special cable that keeps spacewalking astronauts from drifting away from their space vehicle.

thrusters—Clusters of small rockets used to control the movements of a spacecraft.

Further Reading

Books

Chaikin, Andrew, with Victoria Kohl. *Mission Control, This Is Apollo: The Story of the First Voyages to the Moon*. New York: Viking, 2009.

Dyer, Alan. *Mission to the Moon*. New York: Simon & Schuster Books for Young Readers, 2009.

Jefferis, David and Mat Irvine. *Race Into Space*. New York: Crabtree Publishing, 2007.

Kuhn, Betsy. *The Race for Space: The United States and the Soviet Union Compete for the New Frontier*. Minneapolis, Minn.: Twenty-First Century Books, 2007.

Thimmesh, Catherine. *Team Moon: How 400,000 People Landed Apollo 11 on the Moon*. Boston: Houghton Mifflin, 2006.

Internet Addresses

John F. Kennedy Space Center: The Gemini Program
<http://www-pao.ksc.nasa.gov/history/gemini/gemini.htm>

National Aeronautics and Space Administration (NASA): Gemini 4
<http://nssdc.gsfc.nasa.gov/nmc/masterCatalog.do?sc=1965-043A>

Smithsonian National Air and Space Museum: Gemini 4
<http://www.nasm.si.edu/exhibitions/gal100/gemini4.html>

Index